Love Me, Love My Dog!

Written & Illustrated by Keith Robinson

BOWTIE
P R E S S ®

Irvine, California

Karla Austin, Business Operations Manager
Jen Dorsey, Editor
Michelle Martinez, Associate Editor

Rebekah Bryant, Editorial Assistant
Ruth Strother, Editor-at-Large
Nick Clemente, Special Consultant

Library of Congress Control Number: 2004102874
ISBN 1-889540-68-4

BowTie Press®
A Division of BowTie, Inc.
3 Burroughs
Irvine, California 92618

Printed and Bound in Singapore
10 9 8 7 6 5 4 3 2

CONTENTS

INTRODUCTION

OK, so you don't have a dog. There's nothing really wrong with that. Maybe you live in a "no pets" apartment. Maybe you're a "cat person." Maybe you just don't like dogs. Whatever. It's your life.

But at some point, you may find a relationship with a dog unavoidable. Your new romantic interest may share a home with a pooch. Your best friend might take in strays. Your own child may beg for a puppy. For centuries, dogs have been man's best friends. So it's unrealistic to think you can avoid dogs without also avoiding people. Face it. If you are going to lead a normal life, eventually you'll have to deal with the ultimatum, "Love me, love my dog!"

Before you get involved with a dog owner, you are going to have to come to grips with why you've been avoiding dogs. If the problem is insurmountable, it's better to know before you get too attached to the dog owner. No matter how much you may be attracted to him, he isn't going to get rid of the dog to save the relationship. Never say, "It's me or the dog." You'll always lose.

"I'm Allergic"

Allergies to dogs may not seem as common as allergies to cats
(although the cause is the same—proteins in the animals' saliva).
This could be because the proteins are different or the fact that
while cats are pretty much left to wash themselves, most dogs
receive at least the occasional bath. This can reduce the allergens on
the dog. By the way, even though some breeds are considered to be
hypoallergenic, this turns out not to be true—all dogs produce the
proteins to which allergic people react. However, certain breeds are

usually fussed over more than other breeds (i.e. bathed more) and therefore carry less allergens.

So, regular baths for whatever dog you are going to be around may relieve your symptoms. It's just difficult to tell your friends and loved ones that their adorable little poochie isn't clean enough for you.

If your friends do agree to wash Rover more often but your symptoms remain, there are other options: change the surroundings or change yourself.

Change the Surroundings

Even though your sympathetic friends might lock Rover in the garage so that you won't sneeze, these people are in denial about how much shed hair is in the average dog-inhabited house. Just because you can't *see* Rover doesn't mean you are safe from an allergy attack. Plus, you'll still hear Rover's whining and pawing to be let out of the garage. You'll be sneezing *and* feeling guilty.

Some friends knock themselves out vacuuming every square inch of their home just before you come over. This is extremely thoughtful. It also, in many cases, will make things worse. Dander (the too-cute name given to microscopic scales of dried, shed skin) from the pooch carries the proteins you're allergic to. Unless the vacuum cleaner has a very good High Efficiency Particulate Air

(HEPA) filter, it will simply fill the air with microscopic skin particles, creating an invisible cloud of allergens that can last for hours.

If your friends are going to vacuum, it should be the day before you arrive to give that cloud a chance to settle. You can pass this info along to your friends, but, as with telling them to wash their dog, they may not appreciate your passing out housecleaning tips. They probably already have a mother. And vacuum cleaners, even with the most advanced HEPA filters, never make good Christmas, birthday, or anniversary presents. Go figure.

As you become more comfortable visiting friends with dogs, you will likely become open to dating someone with dogs. One day, you

may find yourself in a honest-to-goodness relationship with a dog owner. And, as one thing often leads to another, this relationship may bloom to the point where you are ready to live with a dog owner and, ergo, one or more dogs.

This living arrangement can work by creating an environment to lessen your allergies. The main thing to do is avoid fabrics—no carpets, drapes, or upholstered furniture. While some might consider the suggestion drastic, remember that a few compromises such as hardwood floors and a leather sofa will help you cope. It also helps to designate one room—particularly the bedroom—as a dog-free zone. This is an excellent idea that, in practice, will last about a week.

Change Yourself

There are a number of drugs on the market that can lessen your allergic reaction to dogs. Over-the-counter medications may cause drowsiness. On a romantic visit to a significant other's home, passing out during the salad course is usually the last thing on your mind. Several prescription drugs (and some that have been recently approved to sell over-the-counter) are available that don't cause drowsiness, but they are considerably more expensive. Most of these drugs need to be taken daily to be effective. At these exorbitant prices, you may want to get your *own* pack of dogs just to feel the cost is justified.

If you are going to be moving in with a dog owner, you probably will want to ask your doctor about pills or even allergy shots. But unfortunately, there are fewer treatments for dog allergies than cat, and shots are less effective. Your doctor can advise you best. Ignore the first option he or she recommends, namely getting rid of the pooch. This goes back to never saying, "It's me or the dog." If the second recommendation is getting rid of the relationship, you may want to consider getting rid of the doctor. Let's stick to the *medical* options, Doc.

"I'm Not a Dog Person"

OK, let's be optimistic and say you're not a dog person *yet*.

Maybe you consider yourself a cat person, instead. Why? While there are obvious physical differences between dogs and cats, the real difference—what you are actually responding to—comes down to the animal's senses of humor. Both dogs and cats have a sense of humor, but only a cat can be sarcastic and, some say, cruel just for fun.

Let's say you give a cat some food he doesn't like. The cat may turn up his nose, walk away, pause, then make a little kicking motion with his hind legs, as he does when burying something in his litter box. "Ha! That's what I think of your offering!" you imagine him saying.

A dog would never do that. First, it would be hard to find something he wouldn't eat. And even if you did find something so disgusting the pooch wouldn't eat it, he would probably roll around in it instead, with a big happy "thank you" on his face.

Dogs simply have no sense of irony. Everything is straightforward with them. Theirs is a more clownish, practical joke, pull-my-

finger type of humor. Stealing all your underwear from the laundry and spreading it around the backyard? *That's* comedy.

This lack of the irony gene is what makes dogs so gullible—they're *always* fooled by the fake throw—and so completely accepting of their owners. They love unconditionally. Maybe that's why you don't consider yourself a dog person. Maybe you don't think you deserve unconditional love. Maybe you should see a therapist about that. Or maybe you should just hang out with a dog for a while.

If you didn't grow up with a dog, you may think it would just be too complicated to adjust your lifestyle to include a pooch. Au contraire! As Dr. Spock said about having babies, you already know more than you think you know. And compared with having a baby, having a dog is a walk in the park—literally.

If you are getting close to someone who has a dog, he or she can show you the ropes (or leashes): feeding, walking, picking up after Rover, etc. There are a few things you will have to get used to. For example, with a dog in your life, you can't just get up and go as before. The last-minute romantic getaway or road trip to Vegas isn't happening unless provisions for the dog can be arranged. No piling a heap of dry food in a bowl and taking off, as with a cat. The dog might eat all the food in the first hour, get sick, get mad that you have left him alone, and trash the house. Whoever said, "Hell hath no fury like a woman scorned," never owned a dog that felt, however briefly, abandoned. After all, it's doubtful that even the most scorned woman ever left a "little present" in the middle of the bed just for spite.

On the other hand, there are many times you can take the dog along, unlike with a cat. Many a romantic weekend has been shot down by the phrase, "I'd miss Fluffy too much." With a little forethought, picnics, drives, moonlit walks, and even those romantic weekend getaways, can include Rover.

On the flip side, when you have friends and loved ones with dogs, they will often visit you with pooch in tow. If you live in an apartment with no pets allowed, too many visits may cause a confrontation with the landlord. You may have to resort to sneaking the dog in, perhaps rolled in a carpet or disguised as an ottoman (you corgi fans can pull it off). These tricks will quickly have you evicted

and looking for more dog-friendly housing, which is what you should have done in the first place.

If a dog will be visiting you regularly, you will want to look into dog-proofing your house. This mainly consists of taking everything you own that you don't want chewed, shredded, or drooled upon, and placing it somewhere the dog can't reach, preferably in a storage locker several miles from your home.

No toys for Fido? Don't worry—you'll quickly discover that dogs are pretty much fascinated by whatever humans do. They can sit and watch just about your every move with a look of wonder on their faces. Warning: This can be disconcerting when you are staying at a

loved one's house with a dog for the first time.
The dog wants to see what you do in the bath-
room, wants to watch how you get dressed, and
wants to know what goes on between you and
your loved one.

"Dogs Are Unsanitary!"

Do you cringe when you see a dog owner kiss his or her pet? Does it make you ill if you see a pooch and his master sharing a snow cone? If a dog licks your face do you cry, "Ewww, dog germs!" and run around in circles like Lucy in the *Peanuts* comic strip?

We keep hearing that there are fewer germs in a dog's mouth than in a human's. That's little comfort when poochie's breath lets you know he's been snacking from the cat's litter box again or feasting on his finds from the Dumpster. Speaking of Dumpster, it is true that dogs roll around in rotting garbage. They don't wipe their feet, no matter what they've stepped in. They jump up, putting dirty paws on your clothes. They keep sticking their noses where they don't belong. Some of this behavior can be curbed with training, but some has to be accepted. These are dogs, after all, not Little Lord Fauntleroy.

The question is, where is that acceptance threshold? For someone who has grown up with dogs, it may be fairly high. For you, it may be considerably lower. Your loved one may think nothing of petting the dog, then handing you a dinner roll with the same hand. Or letting the dog rinse the plates with his tongue before they go into the dishwasher. Or kissing the dog, then immediately kissing you. These and other behaviors may be above your personal threshold. If so, the problem will not be training the dog. The problem will be training your loved one. At the same time, of course, your loved one may be trying to train you. If you are going to accept the dog, your loved one may have to accept some limits. But when we mentioned insurmountable problems at the beginning of the book, this may be one of them.

"Dogs Scare Me"

A fear of dogs frequently stems from some incident in childhood, although the occasional news report of someone being ripped to pieces by the neighborhood hound doesn't help.

While deep-seated psychological terror can only be cured by therapy, a fear of dogs may be overcome by getting to know a few of them. Most dogs, when approached openly and with respect, are quite friendly. Of course, you do want to steer clear of dogs that are obviously unfriendly or downright dangerous. Watch for the warning signals of an aggressive, territorial dog. The most obvious of these is a giant "BEWARE OF DOG" sign. Just as clear are the signals the dog himself gives off. While a broad, medium-to-fast sweeping of the tail means a dog is happy to see you, don't take every tail wag as a good sign. A slow wag can mean uncertainty—the dog isn't sure whether to accept you or attack you. A fast wag with the tail held stiff and high is a warning to back off. Beyond wagging, tail position is a good indicator of what the dog is feeling. The tail between the legs shows fright or submission. Lowered but not between the legs shows relaxation. Mostly horizontal but not stiff indicates curiosity. Fully horizontal shows aggression. Tail up shows confidence.

It is best to meet a dog with the owner present, so he or she can reassure poochie that you are an okay person, and can reassure you as well. If the dog is comfortable, you can extend an open hand, palm to pooch (offering the back of your hand can make the pooch curious or nervous about what you are hiding). If the dog sniffs your hand and gives you a friendly tail wag, you can tickle his chest between the front legs. A few such friendly meetings should put you and poochie at ease.

If all such meetings go badly—if dogs always snarl and bark when you get near—maybe the problem isn't your fear of them; maybe they're afraid of you. Possibly you should reevaluate your wardrobe or cologne.

Having a Relationship with a Dog Person

So you met someone special. He or she has a dog, and you think maybe you're ready and willing to accept that. But before getting too involved, you may want to pay close attention to how the pooch behaves, because within six months, you could wind up behaving exactly the same way. Dogs are very sensitive to their owners' personalities and quickly adjust their own behavior in response. While it's fairly easy in the early days of dating for a person to hide their negative side, their quirks and faults may be reflected in their dog.

Is the dog playful and outgoing? This is a good sign as his owner is likely to be, too. But is the dog servile? Is he eager to please but whimpering and groveling when reprimanded? His owner may be domineering. You might be whimpering and groveling soon yourself. Has the dog been trained to do numerous tricks such as roll over, play dead, or sit with a biscuit on his nose? The owner might be a control freak. You might wind up with a metaphorical biscuit on your nose. It should go without saying that if the owner disciplines the dog by striking or beating him, you should not be anywhere near this person; neither should the dog. Does the dog seem anxious or nervous? Look for the owner to be a bundle of nerves him or her-self—and getting on your nerves before too long. On the flip side, don't be too quick to judge a calm, complacent dog as a good sign. More and more neurotic dogs are being prescribed Prozac and other anti-depressants these days. See if you can find out what the pooch is on. Within a few weeks you may want to be on it, too.

Now, to be fair, many dogs have neuroses as a result of breeding or a previous owner. So the dog's behavior may not be entirely due to his owner's personality. This is just a warning. Where there's smoke, there's usually fire.

Types of Dogs

How are you going to get along with your loved one's dog? First, what type is he?

There are over 200 recognized breeds of dogs, broken down into categories such as herding, sporting, guarding, etc. And, of course, there are the mixed breeds and mutts. All have unique temperaments and qualities. However, for the uninitiated (i.e., you), there are essentially three types of dog: small, medium, and large.

The Small Dog

The small dog is about the size of a cat. This is the type of dog carried around in shoulder bags by women in supermarkets and on airplanes. Even among dog lovers, there is some animosity toward these animals, which are frequently dismissed as "yappy little dogs."

To be fair, the yappiness comes about because of their lineage. Most small dogs are descendents of breeds kept for centuries as pets for the aristocracy. They ate caviar and drank champagne while sitting in the laps of the royal children. Think about it. If you were born to eat caviar and drink champagne and instead wound up living in an apartment eating dog food, you'd be yappy too.

On the plus side, these dogs can be quite entertaining. They have no problem trying to boss around people and dogs many times their size. Probably that aristocratic blood, again. On the negative side, these dogs tend to be spoiled by their owners. Be careful getting involved with someone with a small dog. Do they always have the poochie sitting in their

lap? Do they hand feed him while making cooing noises? Do they dress him up? It may be that what they really want is a baby. Do you?

The Medium Dog

The medium dog is about the size of a, well, dog. The medium dog is what we usually think of when we hear the word "dog."

The person with the medium size dog has one because he wants, yes, a dog. For you, the dog neophyte, this is a good situation. The dog is large enough that you are unlikely to step on him and kill him, yet not so large that you'll be dragged down the street when you volunteer to take Rover for a walk.

The Large Dog

The large dog is about the size of a person. He can be intimidating; most people instinctively take a step back when coming face to face with a large dog, which is the idea. Many large dogs are descended from canines bred to guard palaces. They are meant to be imposing, regal, and a bit threatening.

Some people still get large dogs to protect their property, but beware. Some single people, having repeatedly failed at relationships, have opted to get a large dog, whether they know it or not, to protect themselves from intimacy. They've subconsciously chosen a guard dog to guard them from further hurt. They seem open to having a relationship with you, but are unaware that their dog is keeping you away from them. By physically imposing himself between you and your loved one, the large dog makes it difficult to get close emotionally.

And yet, look at the relationship the owner has with the dog. A big dog can be stubborn. When he wants to go one way and the owner the other, it can be quite a struggle. They are always arguing, pulling, and tugging at each other to get their way. In other words, it's like a marriage. So even though the animal is keeping them from forming relationships, what many big dog owners really want is a spouse. Is that what you really want?

Joining the Pack

OK, you've decided that this person and this dog are worth knowing better. You are ready to accept a dog in your life. But is the dog ready to accept you?

The most popular view of how a dog is thinking is the "pack mentality." This theory is that dogs see humans as other dogs. The owner must establish themselves as the alpha dog of the pack.

Some dog experts feel this analogy has been overstretched. They argue that while dogs do drink out of the toilet and can be fooled by bacon-flavored treats, they *can* tell the difference between another dog and a human being. They know their relationship with their master. They know their relationship with another dog. It's you they're not sure of.

Whichever theory is correct, there are three major areas in which you and Rover are going to have to come to terms with in order to get along:

- Territory
- Jealousy
- Authority

Territory

By nature, a dog stakes out and defends his territory, his hunting grounds. If anyone should invade his territory—another dog, a bird, you—his instinct is to protect the area. The first time you show up at your loved one's home, you may be barked or growled at when you enter the yard, enter the door, or enter any new room.

Your loved one will have to vouch for you. Usually, the owner simply introducing you to the dog will signal that it is all right for you to be there. Friendship may take a little more work, though. A doggie treat or two may do the trick. You may try to buy the affection of your loved one's dog by bringing him a new toy. This is not particularly effective. This is how you buy the affection of your loved one's children.

A dog is much more likely to accept you if you take time to play with him. Most dogs will play until the point of exhaustion—yours, not theirs. A dog is always on the lookout for someone who will play and play and play. In other words, he is on the lookout for a sucker. Once you throw that tennis ball for the pooch, he won't let you stop. Try to walk away, and poochie will follow you, carrying that ball in his mouth, trying to guilt you into just one more throw. And the next time you show up, poochie will be right there with that ball in his mouth. You are his ball-throwin' pal.

But don't go overboard. In your efforts to be accepted by your loved one's dog, don't spend so much time playing with him that you neglect to play with your loved one, if you know what I mean. With a proper amount of playtime and attention, the dog should welcome you to the pack!

Jealousy

You're getting along with poochie. He's glad to see you when you come over, he wants to play, and he wags his tail. That doesn't mean there is clear sailing ahead. Jealousy may rear its ugly head—it for you, and you for it.

See, your loved one already has a relationship with his or her dog. Even if the dog accepts you in his territory, he may still try to keep you from physical contact with his owner. This may simply be protecting the master, but it can also be due to sexual jealousy or rivalry.

A male dog can be very possessive of a female owner. Similarly, although usually to a lesser degree, a female dog can be possessive of a male owner. When a human of the opposite sex starts to snuggle up to the master, the dog can feel displaced, upset, and angry. A dog with such feelings may start acting up. He may become destructive, destroying furniture and clothing that he previously left alone. He may urinate or defecate in the house. He may become more aggressive, snarl, or even bite you or others. Cute little Rover may suddenly turn into Cujo.

Or the dog may suddenly feign illness. He may chew his paws or scratch constantly. Dogs have even been known to fake a limp. This drama queen behavior is a cry for attention from the master, even if that attention is anger and discipline. So trying to correct bad behavior may simply reinforce it.

The pooch needs lots of reassurance that he isn't being replaced in the affection of the owner. The owner needs to give lots of love and attention, but not in direct response to the dog's acting up or acting sick.

The owner also has to be careful not to back away from you when the dog starts to get jealous. If the owner starts to shower affection on the pooch while ignoring you, *you* may start to get jealous of the dog. This is not healthy. Speak to your loved one. He or she should not reward the dog's fits of jealousy. In order for you to spend quality time with your loved one, you are going to have to establish your rights to be there. This can't happen unless your loved one backs you up.

And if you feel your loved one is playing you and the dog off each other to keep you both jealous, your problem isn't with the dog. It's probably time to look for a new relationship where manipu-

lation is not involved. But with plenty of attention from you and your loved one, the dog should respect that, sometimes, the two of you will be snuggling alone.

Authority

The last hurdle is authority. The dog may love playing with you and may accept that you and your loved one get to spend time alone together, but he may not accept your authority. The dog recognizes his master as Number One in the household. But who is Number Two?

Although the dog counts you as a member of the pack or family, he may see himself as above you in the pecking order. Even though you may play with him, walk him, and feed him, he may not accept any commands or discipline from you, ignore you, or worse, attack you.

You have to establish your dominance over the dog, but this can only be done with the owner backing your authority. The owner must discipline the pooch whenever he doesn't obey your commands. (Expect some discipline yourself. Follow the owner's lead in how to punish and correct the dog. Do it wrong, and *you* may wind up in the doghouse.)

Your relationship with the dog will be in most ways defined by how the dog sees his owner responding to you. If your loved one's dog doesn't respect you, just how much does your loved one respect you?

Insist that your loved one make poochie understand that you are to be obeyed. Once the new pecking order is understood and respected, you'll be one big happy family.

Let's see where you are now. You set out to accept a dog in your life to get closer to someone you care about. And everything has worked out. You accept the dog and the dog accepts you. But you still may discover a few surprises.

You may find that going for a walk is sometimes more than just a chore; it's a chance for daily meditation, a chance to unwind, a Zen experience, especially once you get used to cleaning up the poop. You may start to look forward to it almost as much as the dog.

When alone with the pooch, you may find yourself venting about little things your loved one does that drive you crazy, and the dog may seem to listen sympathetically. After all, he's been there.

And when you're out of town and you call your loved one, you might ask him or her to put the dog on the phone. Because, well, you miss him.

"Love me, love my dog?"

Face it. You do.

 Keith Robinson has done cartoons and humorous illustrations for a number of publications, including the books *Why Do Dogs Do That?*, *Why Do Cats Do That?*, and *Love Me, Love My Cat!*. His weekly comic strip *Making It: A Survival Guide for Today*, appears in newspapers nationwide and on the Internet at www.makingit.com. Keith is a lifelong resident of Manhattan Beach, California.